What Readers Are Saying

I am enamored by the way you express yourself, S. Swan. The words are filled with both pain and joy which you really made me feel too.

—Carol

I tried not read to all of it but I couldn't stop. :) I loved each one.

It draws you in.
Steals your heart.
Cuts deep into your psyche.
Demands introspection.
Empowers your soul to take a deep breath
and move forward.

From heart-wrenching to inspiring, join multiple writers as they paint a vivid picture of the human experience and take you on a journey of self-discovery, resilience, reflection, and empowerment. This collection is a celebration of the human spirit, and it will leave you feeling inspired, uplifted, and grateful for life's journey.

—K Hubbard

Marble Me Free

The award winning animated short film based on the poem "The Marble Block"

The Marble Block & the Poems It Inspired

S. Swan

ISBN: 978-1-7342991-8-2 (Paperback)
Library of Congress Control Number: 2023905697
First edition March 2023
This book was edited, arranged, and designed by S. Swan
The text was set to 12-point PT Sans

Cover illustration by S. Swan

Print and ebook by Draft2Digital
https://starlitswan.com/

Contents

I looked inside me without fear,
willing to share what I have experienced
for others to heal from my own healing.

S. Swan

The Marble Block

By S. Swan

As I was living my life,
I came across a marble block in my way.

I tried to avoid it,
but I couldn't.

I tried to go around it,
but I couldn't.

I tried to go above it,
but I couldn't.

I tried to go under it,
but I couldn't.

It was too big to avoid,
nor ignore.

It was too wide to go around,
nor rationalize.

It was too sleek to climb,
nor see the end of it.

It was too rooted in the ground,
nor did I have the ability to dig it out.

It blocked my way forward.
It put a stop to my life.
It stopped me.
It trapped me.

It trapped me in a present,
I could not escape.
My past,
I had already lived.
My future blocked.
My dreams crushed.

I was trapped, trapped, trapped...
by this...this block,
so huge it took over my life.
It became my life.

This could not be happening to me,
yet it was.
I screamed at it, "Get out of my way!"
yet it didn't.
All I wanted was to have my life back,
yet I didn't.
I pleaded, "What do you want from me?
Tell me! Just tell me...
is this a test? A lesson I must learn?
A punishment? What?!"

I asked crying over and over,
pounding on the unyielding surface,
never getting an answer.
The answer was not in the marble.
The marble was just that,
marble.
Not a punishment,
not a lesson,
just marble,
nothing more,
nothing less.
I was the one torturing myself
for seeing it for more than what it was.

In anger,
I hit back,
I kicked and punched,
nicking the sleek surface,
hurting and cutting myself in the process.

In desperation,
I cried,
and my tears rolled down the bloodied jagged surface,
so much so it washed away the blood
as the marble started to erode.

Finally, with my back against the block,
to tired to fight,
to tired to feel hope,
I accepted the fact
that I was trapped
by a giant cold unwavering unfeeling marble block.

I looked at my bloody hands
with shards of marble embedded,
and I smiled.

I removed the shards,
and I took the time to heal my hands,
so I could put them to work.

As I sat with my back against the block,
I smiled, gathered myself, and relaxed.
I needed to be in full strength for the work ahead.

I stood up in my inner strength in front of that block
as I struck and chipped that marble block.

I chipped and chipped away
until the sleek surface became rough.

I chipped and chipped away
until it started to take form.

I kept carving my own way through,
chipping at it,
little by little,
making my own path through the marble block.

I found my peace in not wasting my time fighting reality.
In accepting it, I became the sculptor of my life.

“As I was living my life,
I came across a marble block in my way.”

Barriers

By Elayne Lansford

Starlit wrote about facing
an immobile, still barrier.
I just slammed into a
natural and moving one.

The ice storm hit us with fury. I am sitting in a cold house with a generator to keep the lights on. We cannot cook or bathe or wash things, but those are just little indignities, and they will be over soon.

The storm will pass too. By tomorrow, the ice will be gone, but the destruction will not pass. There are hundreds of broken trees. They are my tree friends, the oaks I love and commune with every day.

Some are uprooted, some are snapped in half. Some have crowns splintered off, and almost all have lost limbs, some of them massive. The ground is a sad tangle of oak brush, and green leaves still embedded in ice. We essentially had to chainsaw our way out of our front door to start our cleanup.

We will trim our trees in the coming weeks and leave some of the trunks for snags, where the woodpeckers and the owls may dwell one day. However, there is no doing away with the loss. My lovely shaded yard will not be the same. The huge grove of trees in which we live will have blank spot after blank spot, where once there were protecting limbs and leaves.

This must be how it feels to have been hit by a hurricane.

I was working this morning and heard a deafening crash. A huge branch had fallen and shattered my largest greenhouse, where the giant potted plants and the agaves and succulents wintered. I had lemon trees, giant bird of paradise grown from seed 20 years ago, white agapanthus from the monarch lands of Michoacan, a clone of a sacred cypress in Oaxaca, Peruvian cacti from my late stepmother, violet bottlebrush, giant crinum lilies grown from little bulbs from Hawaii, a tropical crinum spirited away as a tiny shoot from Key West...I had 20 baby Agave Parryii, all grown from my beloved mother agave who perished in Snowmageddon, and a multitude of little succulents and cacti.

The greenhouse was a broken shell with the top sheared away, and a giant broken branch in the middle, covering everything with ice and frozen leaves. One cannot fight nature. I know that well, but I also knew that I still had a chance to save my plants, if I moved quickly. I put on four layers of shirts and coats, two layers of pants, two layers of socks and gloves and went out to save whatever I could. For two hours, I pulled ice and branches off and saved every plant I could carry. My house filled with little plants, a bit shocky, but not dead. Being able to do something helped a lot, though after a while my hands and feet began to freeze, and my clothes got soaked through by the melting ice. I am older now, and my little body sways under heavy weight and extended lifting. However, I just kept on. I had to.

Once the smaller plants were safe in the house, my husband helped me throw tarps over the plants too huge to move, who would have had no place to go even if I could move them. We had one wall and two corners of the greenhouse still standing and hoped the walls and the tarps could still keep the big plants alive.

I hate global warming, which I believe has caused this. However, I cannot hate nature. She is impartial, and often as abundant as she is destructive. It is just what it is.

So I have to find my comfort in having saved all that I could. We will rebuild the greenhouse, and plants will be able to live there again. As for the big ones so unprotected now, I do not know their fate. At my age, I have lost many things. I am sad, but also know that nothing lasts forever.

Some of what I dreaded most has occurred, but I am still standing, aching, but unbowed otherwise. Grief will be my territory for a while, but then it too will change.

In the house, by the scores of rescued plants, are the seeding flats with their lights above and heat mats below. Even in the face of the outer destruction, there are zebrinas, Tahoka daisies, Lindheimer's indigo, and pink salvias peeking their tiny selves above the soil in the flats. It won't be the same, but life will still go on. I let that cycle sweep me up, and know there will be joy and life again, even with all that is broken around us.

this heart rises

Melanie Alberts

this heart rises
   petal by petal by
   your tender palm

this heart rises
petal by petal by
your tender palm
melanie alberts

"I tried to go around it,
but I couldn't.

I tried to go above it,
but I couldn't.

I tried to go under it,
but I couldn't."

Trapped?

By Paul Causey

Is the wall before me real?
Is it blocking where I want to go?
Perhaps the impediment is not the block,
but the eyes by which it is seen.

Does the block need to change?
Is that something I can do?
Perhaps the impediment is not the block,
but the beliefs by which it is perceived.

There is pain, so much pain,
whether real or not, it's just the same.
Perhaps the impediment is not the pain,
but the fear that I feel, so much fear.

Am I strong enough, brave enough to change
the eyes by which I see,
the beliefs by which I perceive?
In pain, can I be set free?
Can I change the world that belongs to me?

Yes, I can. You showed me how,
and what to believe in now.

How Do I Get Around This?

By Ivory Danay Smith

A marble wall, a block, an obstacle,
  or is it a resting place?

  I cannot move forward,
  or around it,
  but I must acknowledge it
  because it is blocking my view.

  Where I once saw sky, blue and bright
  I now see cold, milky stone,
  Beautiful yet unbending.

  As I stare, I become helpless.
  Then, anger takes over
  as I scream to the sky.
  "God, why this?
  What did I do to deserve this?"

An energy block can be heavier
than the real thing sometimes.
Shocks, they feel like lightning,
searing through my core,
ripping me apart
as an eon of pain and grief
seeks to escape from within me.

A sleeping monster,
seeking to be free.
Tame until now.

I twist against the shackles of chains
bound around my feet, hands, and neck,
yelling at the stone,
cursing it,
wishing it would disappear.

And yet, it is still here.
My words bounce off it with ease,
unwelcome.

So I cry,
and cry some more
until I can't.

I am weary.
I find peaceful sleep
as I rest against the smooth surface.

When I awake,
it is still here,
but a hammer and chisel appear.

Tools.
Ways to cope.
I can turn this into a masterpiece,
or chisel through until I get to the other side.

Either way,
it is all up to me.

“It trapped me in a present,
I could not escape.
My past,
I had already lived.
My future blocked.
My dreams crushed.

I was trapped, trapped, trapped...
by this...this block,
so huge it took over my life.
It became my life.”

Inhale

By Jenille Cross-Figueroa

I can't move...

Labored inhale.
Breathe Jay, just breathe.
You've got this!

I feel the walls of my life closing in on me,
making me smaller and smaller.
I'm collapsing into myself...
I am a black hole.

Days flow into each other.
I take long routes to get home,
my life is slowly killing me.

My feet are mired in quick sand...
Panic panic panic...
Hyperventilating.
Breathe Jay, just breathe.

Something's gotta give,
I don't want it to be me...
I'm spiraling...

What do I do?
Sit awhile,
think.

Mmm...sweet oblivion.
This is nice.
Deep inhale.
I can breathe.
Free inhale.
This is nice.

Psst,
who's there?
Life.
Okaaaay...
What's up?
You know you can change things, right?

Inhale.
Thinking thinking thinking...
Where do I begin?
Inhale.

Open mind.
Open heart.
What's one thing you've always wanted to do
but you've been scared to do?

Thinking.
Mmm...good,
that's real good.

Now, go do it!

Okay,
deep inhale.
Slow exhale.
Free.

Beyond

By Peggy Lamb

To stand alone on the Ross Ice Shelf
  in the Arctic winter
  where earth and cosmos meet.

  So cold,
  to stand alone in perfect darkness.
  So cold,
  the human body cannot bear it.

    The woman in the teal shroud creeps,
    exhaling ice breaths.
    Trillions of ice gusts!
    But the glacier still melts.

    She gazes up at the moon of ice
    which gazes back in wordless consciousness,
    unconcerned and neutral about rising sea levels.

    If she had this neutrality,
    she would comprehend the word serenity.
    Instead,
    she weeps from the hurt locker her body has become.
    What a dolphin's body has become.

    The pain that reaches for ice each night.
    "Let me live in the region of ice," she prayed,
    and so she creeps for a thousand nights.

Until tumbling into the frigid waters of the Weddell Sea,
mates with a leopard seal
to reclaim her selkie self

Return to her water home.
Let the hurt locker heal.
Seawater as blood, nourishing and transmuting her cells.
Signals of safety sent along neural circuits,
spinning, diving, twisting, spiraling,
liquid dancing her future self.

    Floating,
    gazing at Venus,
    melting into Neptune,
    knowing peace.

Bound

By Bianca Bedugno

tears banging on my eyes
from the outside in
words unable to form
ripping at each other

movement halted
images words sounds
spinning around and around

clanking my brain
stuttering my heart
emptying my soul

nothingness appears
everything surrounds me
light dark
hot cold

balanced unbalanced
breaking me
breaking worlds

particles splitting open
molecules dancing across the sky
up
up
up

stop
stop
stop

let me out

feel   the pain   of another
not as them   but as you
their pain   is yours   forgotten
     crinkled up   and stuffed   in your pocket

lay it out   gently   across   your forehead
 for all   to see
its beauty

you are now human
one with one

"This could not be happening to me,
yet it was.
I screamed at it, 'Get out of my way!'
yet it didn't.
All I wanted was to have my life back,
yet I didn't.
I pleaded, 'What do you want from me?
Tell me! Just tell me...
is this a test? A lesson I must learn?
A punishment? What?!'"

The Well and Me

By Melissa K. Tolliver

For me, the marble block came in the form of a well, a well of illnesses. Just as I felt I could accomplish something that would let me bring creativity into the world, finish a project, pay the bills, help my family...I would be picked up and thrown into the well.

It was wet and damp. The sides were made of brick. The bucket was way above my head. When I looked up, sometimes I would see the sky, sometimes I would hear my children cry, sometimes the sky would be black and the silence deafening. I was tired, I wanted to ignore my life. Just hide, not forever, just for a while.

My mother told me, "if you would just learn the lessons the Universe is trying to teach you, you will stop getting sick." Over and over, she asked me, "What do you think that lesson is?"

Finally, I screamed at her, "Sometimes the Universe looks away, and you just get a bum body!"

I fantasized that I was a changeling. I was only supposed to be here till I was three when I died on an operating table, but chose to come back. All the rare illnesses were a result of my body not being prepared to grow up in human form.

Later in life, the attacks caught me by surprise. I read (luckily well after I had survived one) that there was only a 30% survival rate. My children got used to playing by my hospital bed. They learned, among other things, compassion. My oldest son brought me his security stuffed duck to mend. Then he said, "I thought...maybe you should keep it to help you get better." That act filled and broke my heart at the same time.

People can only deal with someone's pain and suffering for a limited amount of time. I tried to be upbeat. Look to the future. One day, I confided to my best friend that I didn't think I could make it out of the well one more time. I just wanted to crawl into bed and stay there. Not do myself in (bad Karma you know), just retreat. I saw a look in her eyes, saying she couldn't cope with that choice. When she went home that day, I knew she wouldn't be back for a long time.

I had an amazing doctor who did research and found me a drug that kept me out of the hospital. Of course, that was wonderful, but the damage to my life was done...the lost time with my husband and the kids, my house was falling apart, and this body of mine keeps coming up with new things that only one in a million people have.

While I was down in that well, I learned to levitate enough that I could grab the bucket and hold on until someone, angel or human, would start tugging, helping me out of the well. But sometimes that someone had to be me...climbing the rope, grabbing onto the rim...freedom within reach....Feeling a rush of adrenalin propelling me over the side to stand, firmly on the ground.

The Swinging Pendulum

By Kim Mosley

Most of my time I'm wishing that things
will go well. the rest of the time I worry
that they won't. of course, since I'm often
either not or barely in control, this is a
big waste of a Life. Both of my parents
had Legitimate stuff to worry about. And
there is no doubt that the fodder for worry
abounds. But isn't there a road that isn't
fraught with senseless worry? What might
be more productive? What might be more
fun? What might give someone a little
Less suffering? I guess I can depend on
things sometimes not going well. Can I
simply celebrate the swinging pendulum?

My North Star

By Jean Lopez

It isn't true for me
that in accepting reality,
I became the sculptor of my life.

For what is my reality?
This changing flux
from moment to moment.

Or, does my reality
simply mean
the ground under my feet now?

I can't change the past.
I can't predict
or peer through
the dense fog of my future,
and the present
moves at varying speeds.

Feelings do their see-saw dance.
Relationships grow, regress
and maybe flourish to new heights
or fracture.

So the sculptor of my being is really not a solid construct,
or a fixed mass.
It's a glimmer
that can glow dazzlingly bright,
or so faint,
one has to peer to see the embers.

But it's there,
and its constancy
is my north star.

“In anger,
I hit back,
I kicked and punched,
nicking the sleek surface,
hurting and cutting myself in the process.”

Indestructible

by Jess Godwin

Thank you for shifting that boulder of marble,
now I've seen it can be done.

I've always had a hope,
an inkling,
but then the rockslides and cave-ins occur.
Oh, the cavernous tunnels I've dug,
hoping to see light again.

Rock,
so immovable,
seemingly indestructible.
Thank goodness for the wearing and tearing of wind and water.

You will change,
I command it.
I demand it!
I am the only indestructible element.

Will I be like a warm blade slicing butter?
No.
I'm never that smooth.

I was forged before you,
my wound,
my seemingly indestructible foe.

I will shatter you into a million pieces
like you did to me,
only you won't be reassembled.

I won't chisel or carve you.
I will pound you endlessly into dust
and melt you down.

Only then, can I recreate my suffering
and transformation,
transcending into glass
into a shiny fragile object.

How beautiful and desirable
vulnerability is,
something you could never grasp.
You never will,
seemingly indestructible you.

“Finally, with my back against the block,
to tired to fight,
to tired to feel hope,
I accepted the fact
that I was trapped
by a giant cold unwavering unfeeling marble block.”

Through a Locked Door

By Sarah Webb

A door is locked, the way forward blocked. The life we hoped for, gone. It's everywhere. A friend who has lost the love of her life, another who is dying, her sister who cannot remember what she said a moment before...The pain of endings, of change. It is scary, no matter how bravely we meet it.

In my own time of deep suffering, I denied. I could not face the reality. It took me a long time--years--to face the truth. When I did, there was no immediate release. I had to turn to the pain, the loss--to grieve and to grow stronger, to accept help. The life I made was not the life I had planned. I had to let go of that old life.

And if we are dying?

My friend lies in her bed. She can no longer leave it, cannot even turn on her side. She can see out to her driveway, watch TV, talk with visitors. She speaks matter of factly about her death...wonders how long she will have to wait. She says she is ready, wishes she could go on and die, even though she doubts if she will continue past her death. But she sat up, intensely interested, when I spoke of relatives who died in peace, who tried to share the rightness of what they were experiencing. A grandfather who whispered, "Happy days are here again." A grandmother who drew a circle in my cousin's palm. My mother's shining gaze. Still, for my friend this time of dying is her new life. Perhaps something lies past, but that is not the way she thinks about it.

Can we begin again in the days of our dying? Perhaps. We can live our life fully, reach out to those we love, as best we can. My friend has people she cannot forgive, but I see how she accepts her extreme limits and how she tries to help her daughter, who is caring for her and a sick husband at the same time. She eats the food that is cooked for her and does not say anything if she doesn't like it. She accepts pain and times of isolation without complaint. She makes a joke of naming the knotholes in the ceiling. She is going into a week of respite care, even though she doesn't want to, because she knows her daughter needs her to.

My friend is living her best life as she can. And when death itself comes, I hope that she—and all of us—will walk past the loss through yet another doorway.

Gift

By Ksenia Alessandra Petrova

how do i go on living
  when feeling crushed by reality
  again
  and again?

  what is there
  in me
  that wants to live so desperately
  that i endure
        and endure
        and holds my being
  despite knowing
  that this ache
        this anguish
  (most probably)
  will be my companion
  in every moment
  of every day of my life?

  what is there in me
  that wants to live
                      love
                      breathe
  despite the torture of not being able to be who i am?

but who am i?

there is this petrifying thought
that i cannot crystallize in my mind.

my mind
is a reality of its own.
my mind
is like a prison.
a maze
so elaborate,
so intricate
like a Borges' short story.

here,
i've been dreaming
for countless centuries
that i am a powerless human being.

here,
the air is dusty
and hot
like the air of the Great Thar Desert.

i remember
being lost
with you
amidst Her sands.

there were three of us,
you
me
and the old cameleer.
in the candent midday,
we found an oasis
and refuge
under a strong baonli tree.

there,
i was laying on the ground
on the layers and layers

of blankets made of camel-yarn
(my soul's in pain,
yet my body's lifeless,
numb from pain
—boca arriba—
facing up)
watching the fight
of two iguanas
for the top spot in the tree.

every breath was filling me
with the glowing
        smoldering
        molten ore of my fears
(mined from the very depth of my being).

i remember
the same blankets
spread all over
Her sands
on one of Her barkhans
(or dunes
as you would call them)
at midnight,

and me,
begging to be free...
to be free from this pain,
not being able to bear
this agony any more,
screaming,
"enough!
i don't want to be enchained
to this misery,
nor
do i want to multiply it!"

the old cameleer stretched out
his hand to me
with a gift from his people,
a gift from Her.

i remember
my firm
clear and conscious
decision
to face my fears
—all of them—
one by one,
slowly,
deliberately
de uno en uno.

i remember
how each of these fears
was becoming smaller
                                        harmless
                                        insignificant
till everything
became one
swaying ocean of love.

i remember being dissolved
in its waters
under the shimmering lights of distant stars.

i remember
all of us being me,
and Her
also being me,
and the pain being me,
and the one who was causing pain
being me.

everything being me.

and just like that
                    magically
                    inexplicably
there was no more pain,
nor fear
when i finally felt my body again.

since then, i continue
(being? living?)
knowing now
that i'm coming from a place of love.
the same place,
i'm going to return to one day.

it just took me sometime
(and some courage)
to un-dis-remember it...

"As I sat with my back against the block,
I smiled, gathered myself, and relaxed.
I needed to be in full strength for the work ahead."

Opening

By Mylene Zozaya Tinoco

One day, I engaged in my mudra, and I was finally able to open[1] a crack in my astonished marble cube.

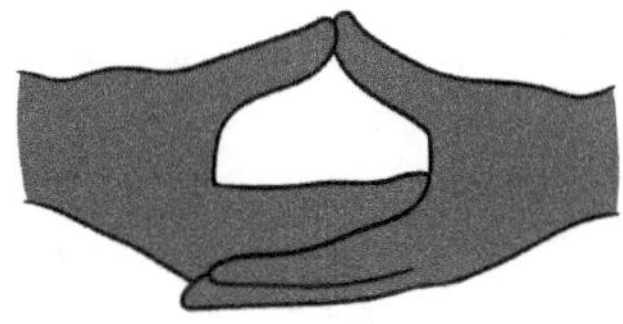

A mudra is a hand position used in Buddhism during meditation. The image above is the "cosmic mudra".

---

1. Awaken to life as it is.

"I stood up in my inner strength in front of that block as I struck and chipped that marble block."

The Debris of My Efforts

By Lucinda Wise

Chip chip!
Collecting pieces,
placing them in a glass basket
to use again and not waste.

My tools grow larger,
the pieces heavier,
and the sounds more forceful.
I smile and lift and place carefully.

Sharp metal sounds,
creating breaking sounds.

With effort, I puuush.
Soon, I can not lift,
shoving sounds
cease.

Leaning on the debris
as it presses against me,
I think heavily,
should I begin again?

Can I begin again?
Am I able?
Do I have what it takes to persevere?

Should I...?
What is the purpose?
Am I getting where I want to go?

“I found my peace in not wasting my time fighting reality. In accepting it, I became the sculptor of my life.”

Perspective

By Veda Smith

Confucius said three things will destroy any society: insolent children, adults who fail to set a good example, and old people who refuse to die.

At eighty five, it's possible I am guilty on all three counts. But wait! I can still shout out the good news of poetry, how it can delight the insolence out of some children, how it can instruct on setting good examples, and as for being old? Just throw enough good poetry at me, and I'll die happy.

Thank You

By S. Swan

People told me,
I had a seed growing in me.
I shed it through my tears.

People encouraged me to plant it,
I did so digitally.

The seed sprouted
letters, words, sentences,
roots.

It grew into a flower,
into a poem,
into a film,
into this
book.

It bloomed from me as a gift,
as a scream,
as a stream of tears.

It showed me my resilience,
my hope,
my willingness to live,
to reach out.

It reflected the beauty of life,
my delight of being alive,
my cherish of you in my life.

I picked the flower
that grew from the seed
you saw in me,
and now I offer it
to you freely.

Also By S. Swan

How Reindeer Learn How to Fly
(Illustrated book)

Anything Is Possible
(Illustrated book)
Book Release April 23th, 2023

About the Author

S. Swan is a writer at heart. She writes poems, short stories and is writing her first novel. She uses writing to create wondrous worlds to escape the pain from Complex Regional Pain Syndrome (CRPS). She is trying to take away the stigma of talking about pain—physical and emotional.

The Marble Block started as a poem. It was made into the award winning animated film "Marble Me Free". And now, it has evolved into a poetry therapy workshop that addresses the reality that physical pain can be the source of emotional pain as emotional pain the source of physical pain. It is not pretty, it is not easy, and it takes courage as she has experienced by breaking through her marble block and allowing her golden flower to bloom.

Acknowledgments

Thank you Kim for green lighting this project, helping me get everyone on board, and for your advice. Thank you to each and everyone of you in Zen Writing for inspiring me, encouraging me and for being part of this project. Thank you Diane & Lucia, my Marble Me Free teammates, for your unwavering support. Thank you Melissa for helping me by reading this book to me, for your emotional support and for letting me bug you at all hours with the most outlandish questions, and Ken for putting up with it. Thank you Kendi for your marvelous talent. Thank you Alana for giving me access to a fountain of creativity. Thank you Bryan for sharing what I do. Thank you Sylvia for supporting and believing in me. Thank you Terry, Becky, and Lucinda for believing I could. Thank you Mirna for helping me in the process to distinguish truth from lies, so I could publish this book just because I wanted to.

www.ingramcontent.com/pod-product-compliance
Lightning Source LLC
LaVergne TN
LVHW050609100826
845148LV00015B/3195

* 9 7 8 1 7 3 4 2 9 9 1 8 2 *